manga moods

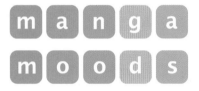

saori takarai

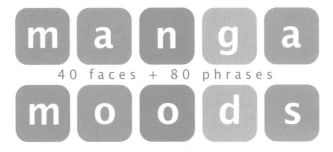

manga

40 faces + 80 phrases

moods

MANGA
UNIVERSITY®

Gift Books

TOKYO SAN FRANCISCO

Manga Moods: 40 Faces + 80 Phrases
By Saori Takarai

Published by Manga University under the auspices of Japanime Co. Ltd.,
3-31-18 Nishi-Kawaguchi, Kawaguchi-shi, Saitama-ken 332-0021, Japan.

www.mangauniversity.com

Editor: Glenn Kardy
Art director and designer: Shinobu Sendai

Special thanks to Mari Oyama and Ron Morse.

No manga characters were harmed in the making of this book.

ISBN-13: 978-4-921205-13-3
ISBN-10: 4-921205-13-2

10 9 8 7 6 5 4 3   y 15 14 13 12 11 10 09 08 07

Printed in China.

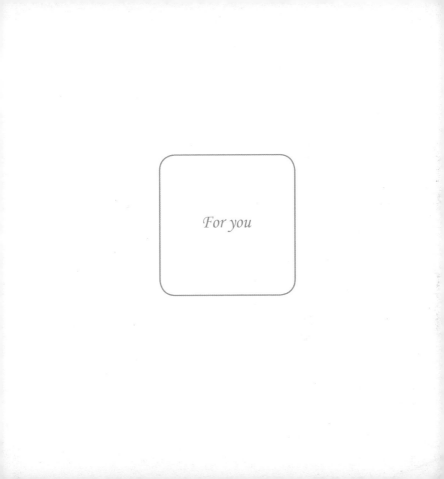

For you

table of contents

foreword

A raised eyebrow, a curled lip, a wink of the eye. All it takes is a clever stroke of the G-pen to instantly change a manga character's mood from one extreme to the other: glad to sad, sneaky to shy, angry to embarrassed. In *Manga Moods: 40 Faces + 80 Phrases,* Saori Takarai presents a series of full-color drawings to show just how these transformations take place.

In addition, each of the facial expressions is labeled with the English and Japanese words for the mood being depicted, along with Japanese conversational phrases and their translations. The phrases are romanized for easy learning, and at the back of the book you'll find handy charts of the hiragana phonetic alphabet that you can use to transcribe the romanized words into authentic Japanese writing.

Much more than a collection of cute characters, *Manga Moods* provides you a fresh new way of looking—and laughing—at life.

notes

For the convenience of our readers, the phrases in this book have been romanized rather than written in traditional Japanese script. We have used a simplified form of the Hepburn method of romanization, the same system that is used by the Library of Congress in the United States and many governmental agencies in Japan. Words are spelled in a way that allows English speakers to pronounce Japanese with ease.

The Japanese language has five vowels:

a as in ah   *i* as in we   *u* as in soon   *e* as in get   *o* as in old

Long vowels are written as aa, ii, uu, ē and ō in this book.

Consonant sounds are virtually the same as those heard in English, with the following notable exceptions. The "f" sound is considerably softer in Japanese than in English. And the "l" sound is almost nonexistent in Japanese, with a Japanese approximation falling somewhere between a "d" and an "r" to English-trained ears, and romanized with an "r."

Energetic
かっぱつ Kappatsu

Hajimemashite!

Nice to meet you!

Hajimemashō!

Let's begin!

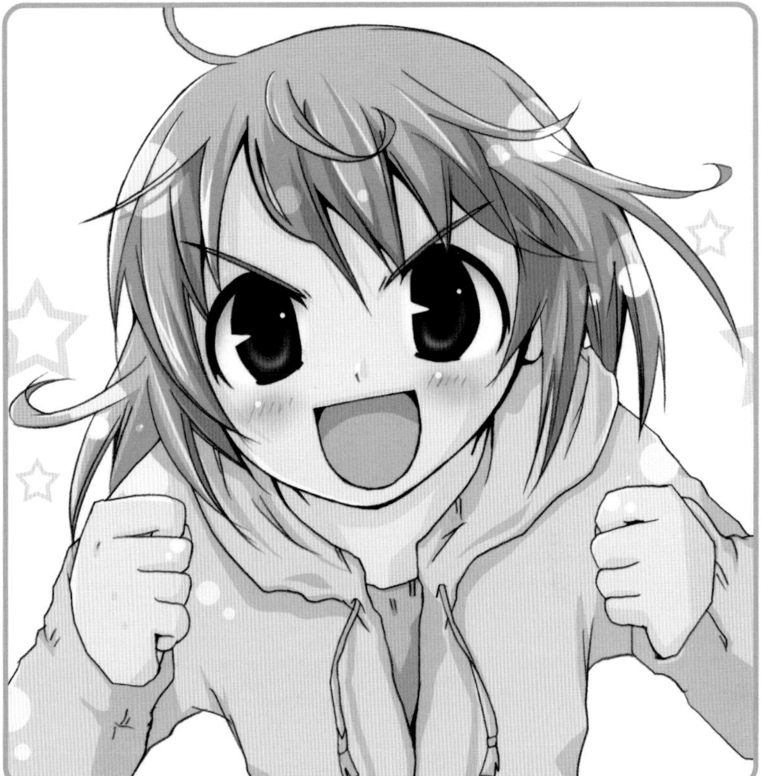

Grumpy
きむずかしい Kimuzukashii

Suneteru no?

Sulking?

Sunetenai yo!

I am *not* sulking!

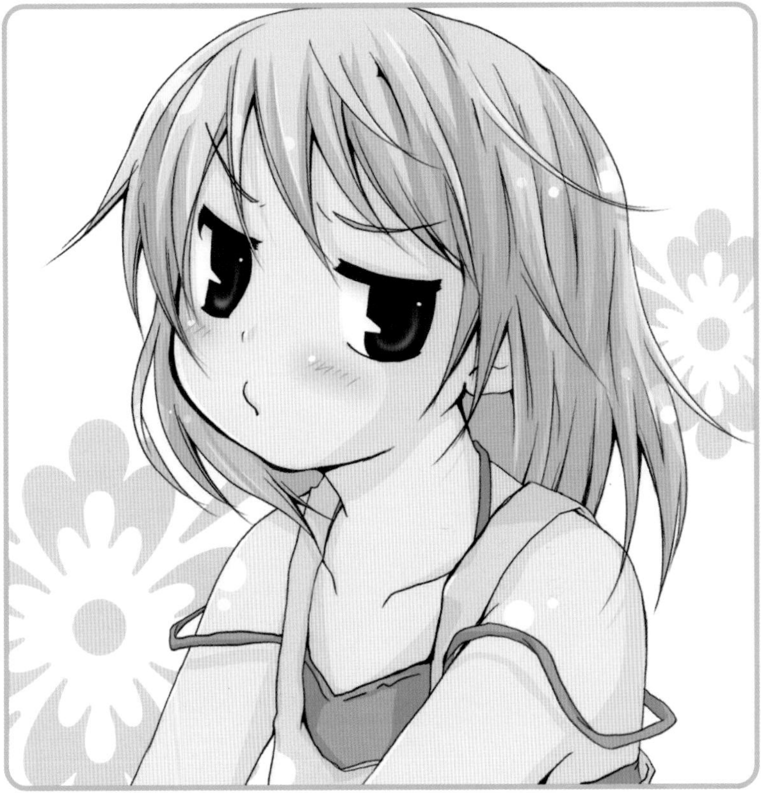

Giddy

おかしい Okashii

Okashi-sugiru!

That's too funny!

Warai ga tomaranai!

I can't stop laughing!

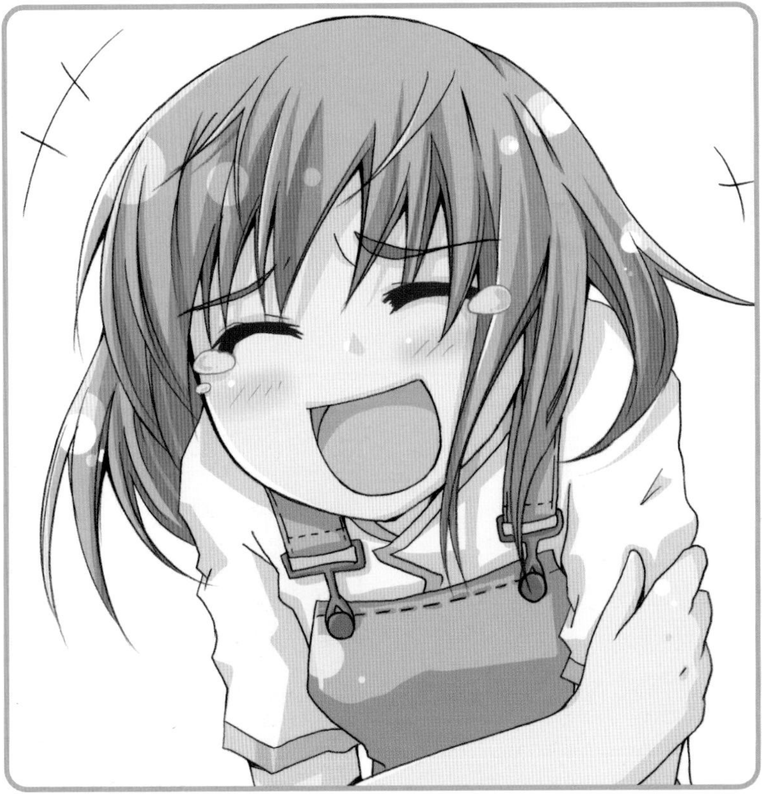

Tearful

かなしい Kanashii

Sugoku kanashii! I'm so sad!	Namida ga tomaranai! I can't stop crying!

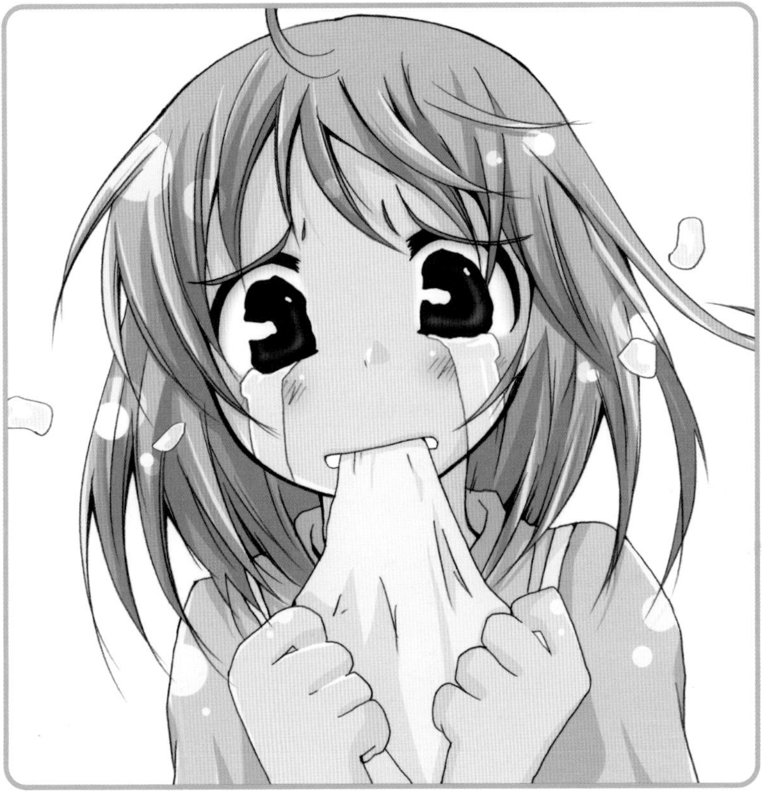

Suspicious

うたがわしい Utagawashii

Watashi no koto
sukina no?

You like me?

Honto ni?

Really?

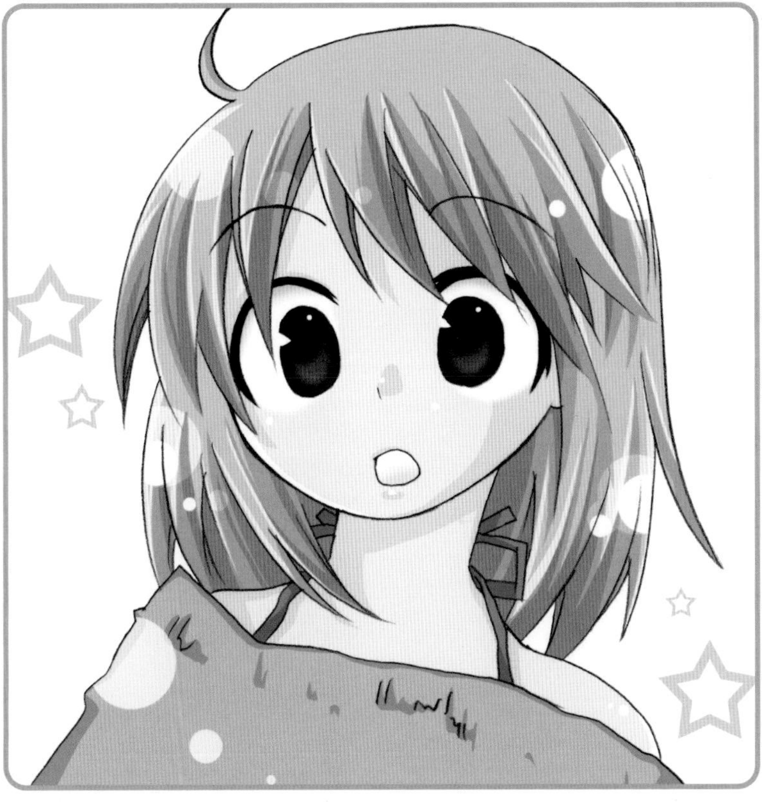

Irritable

いや Iya

Kyō wa
getsuyōbi ka.

Today is Monday.

Getsuyōbi kirai!

I hate Mondays!

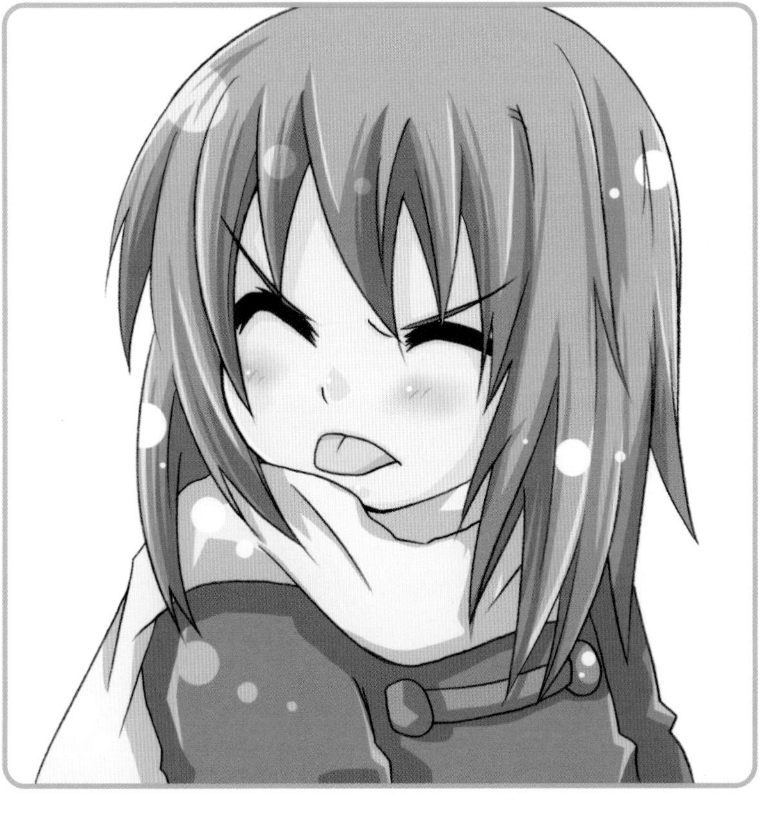

21

Concerned

しんぱい Shimpai

Anata no koto
shimpaina no.

I'm worried about
you.

Daijōbu?

Is everything OK?

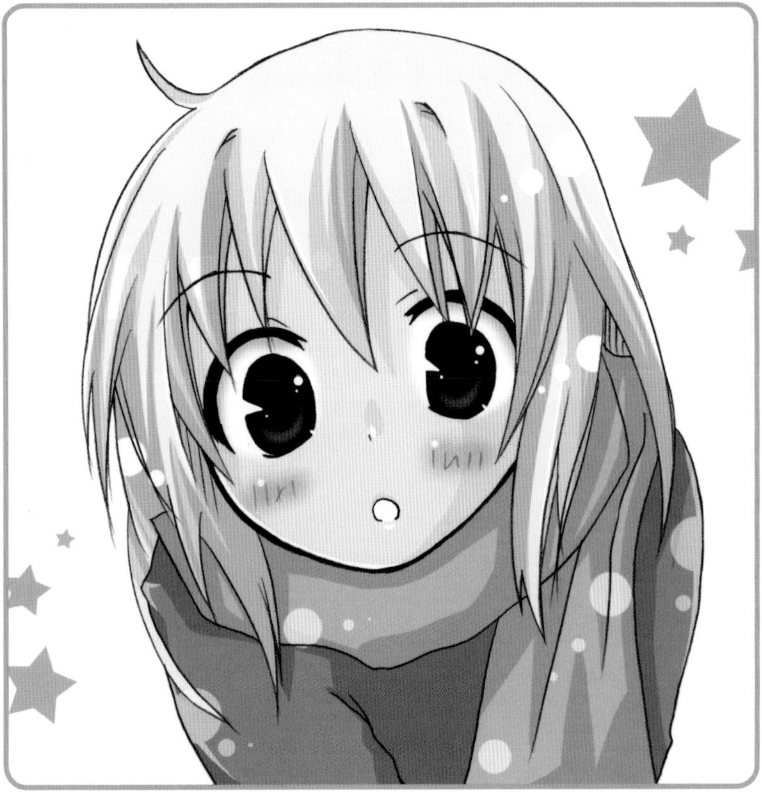

Frightened

こわい Kowai

Obake o mita!

I saw a ghost!

Uwaa!

Yikes!

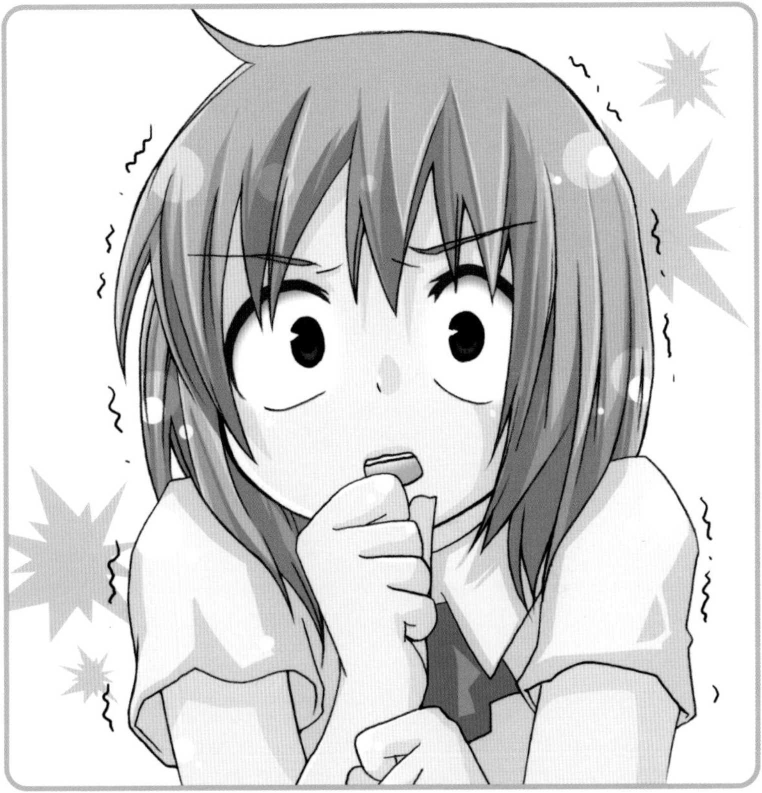

Confused

とまどう Tomadō

Watashi no koto sukina no... He loves me...	Soretomo chigau no. He loves me not.

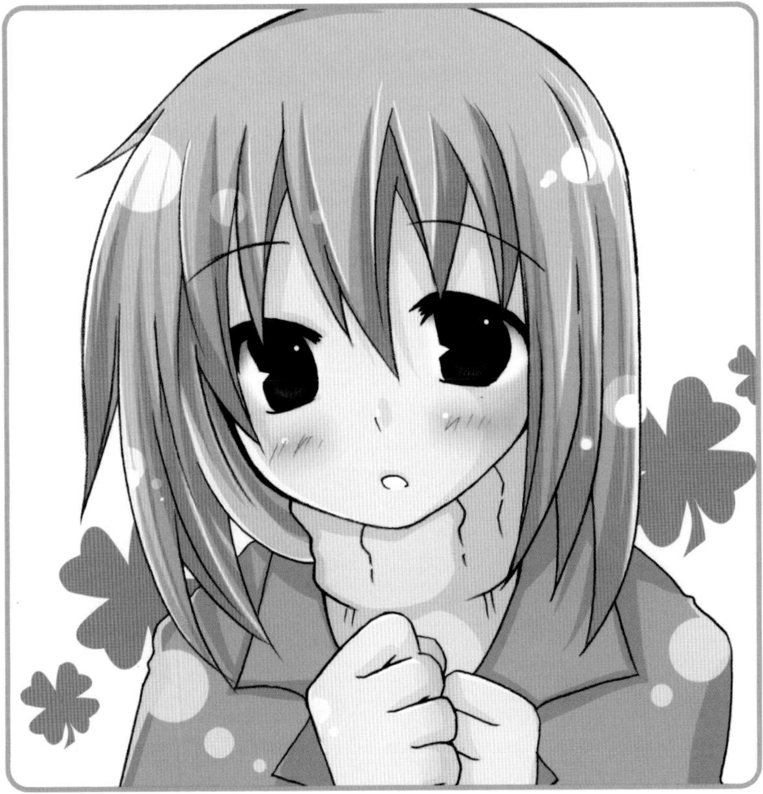

Bewildered

あわてる Awateru

Mayochatta!

I'm lost!

Dochi ni
ikeba ii no?

Which way should
I go?

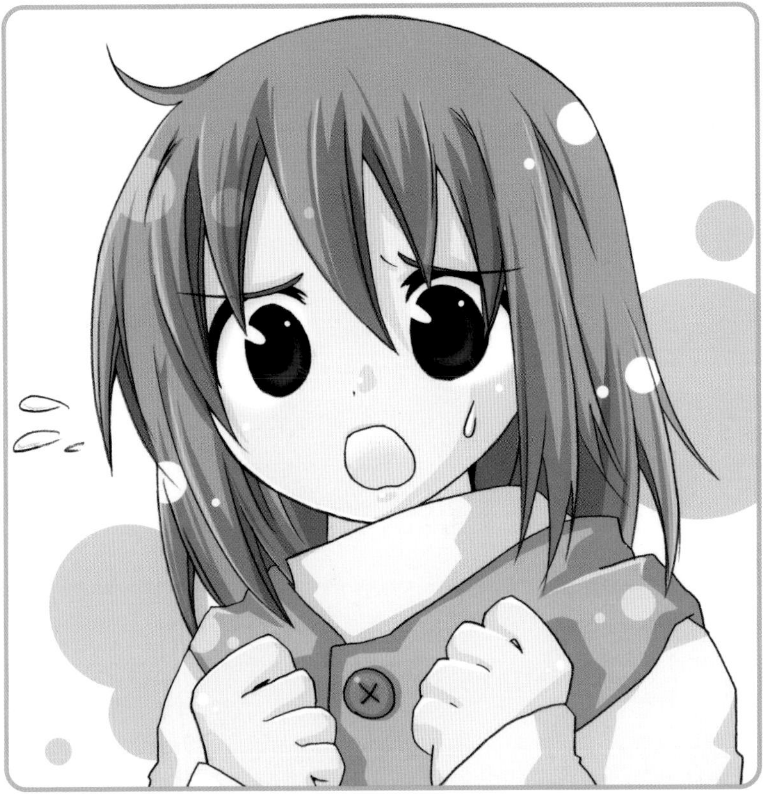

Confident

じしん Jishin

Jibun o
shinjiru wa.

I believe in
myself.

Watashi nara
dekiru!

I can do
anything!

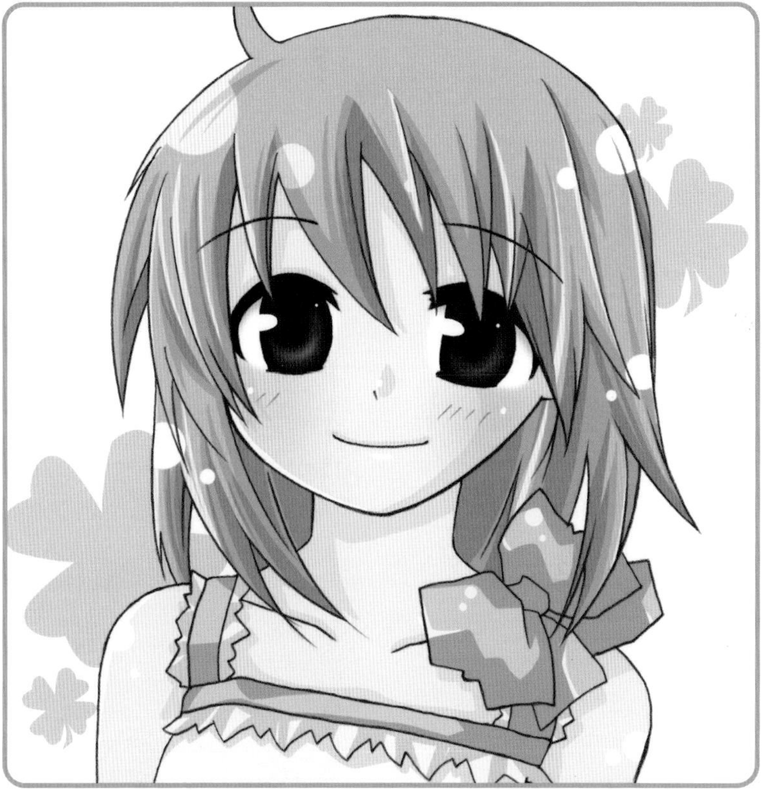

Sad

せつない Setsunai

32

Itteshimatta no ne. He's gone.	Sayōnara. Farewell.

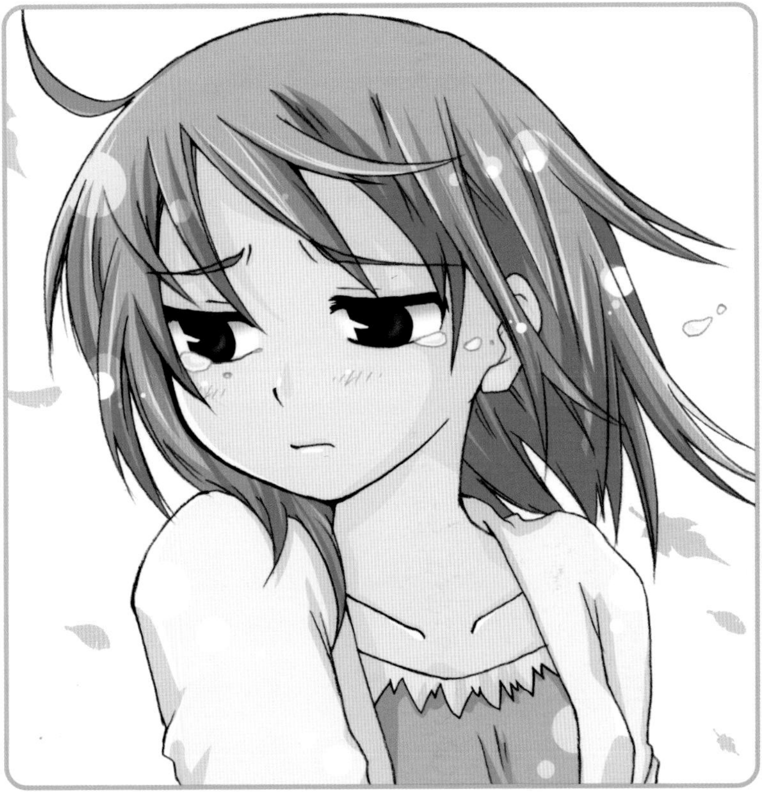

Satisfied

まんぞく Manzoku

Shiawasesō da ne.

You look happy.

Watashi mo ureshii yo!

And that makes *me* happy!

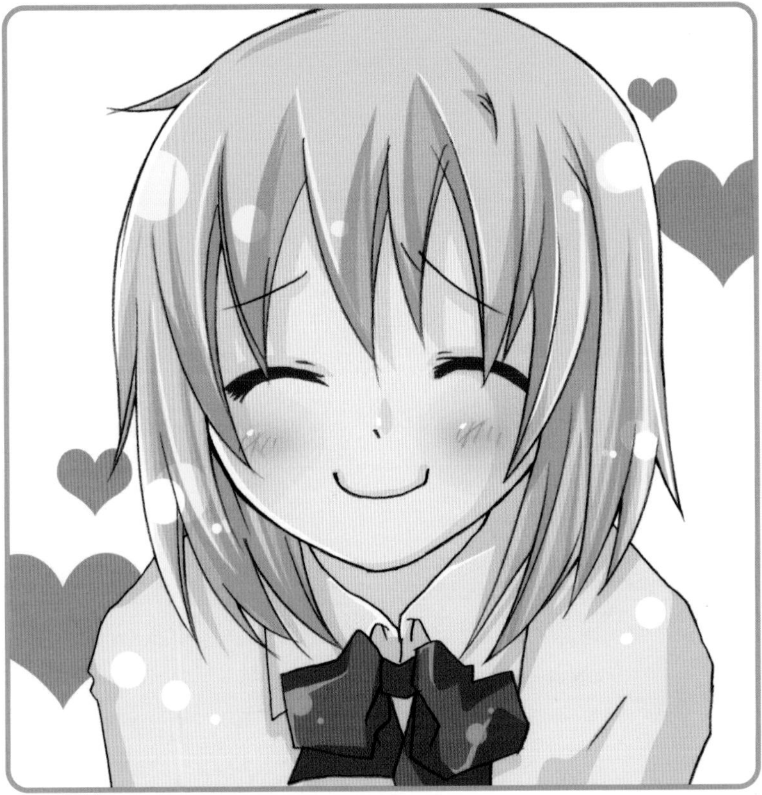

Coy

わざとらしい Wazatorashii

36

Watashi no toshi?

Sore wa himitsu!

My age?

It's a secret!

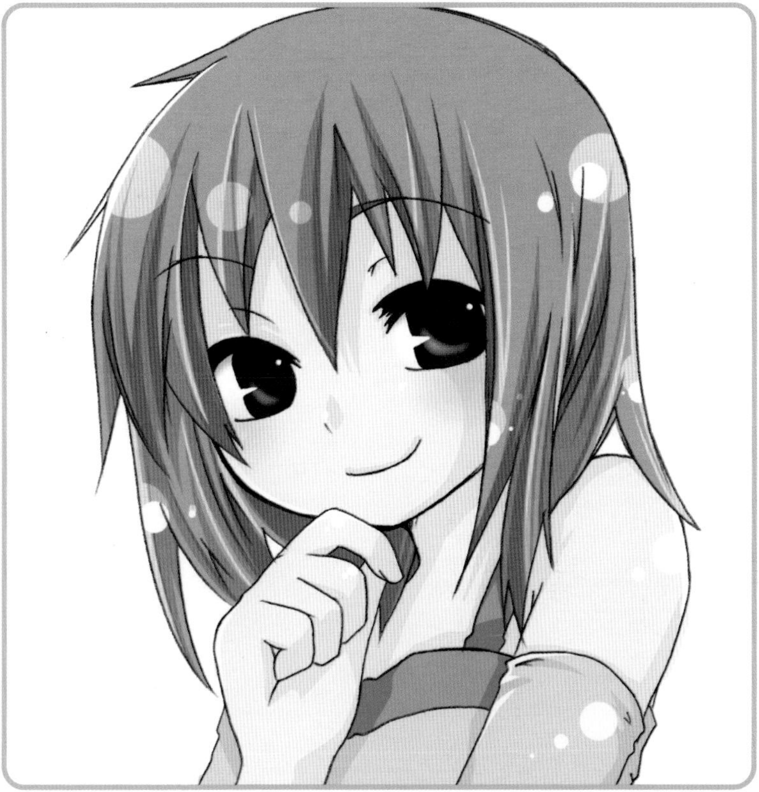

Apprehensive

やばい Yabai

38

Ēto...	Toire wa doko?
Ummm...	Where's the bathroom?

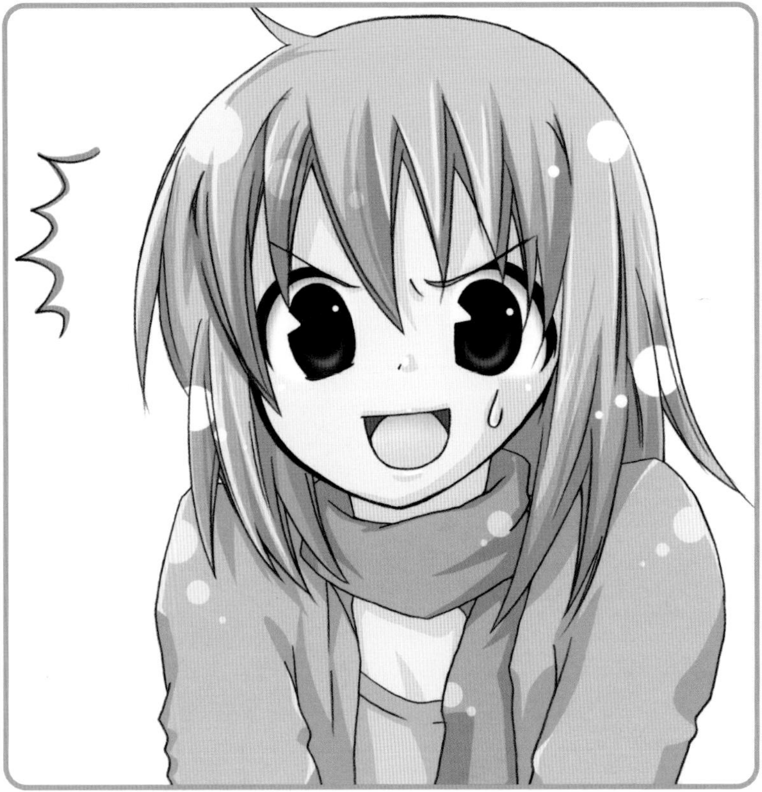

Defiant

ちょうせんてき Chōsenteki

Watashi to
anata ga?

You and *me?*

Nani itteru no yo!

Dream on!

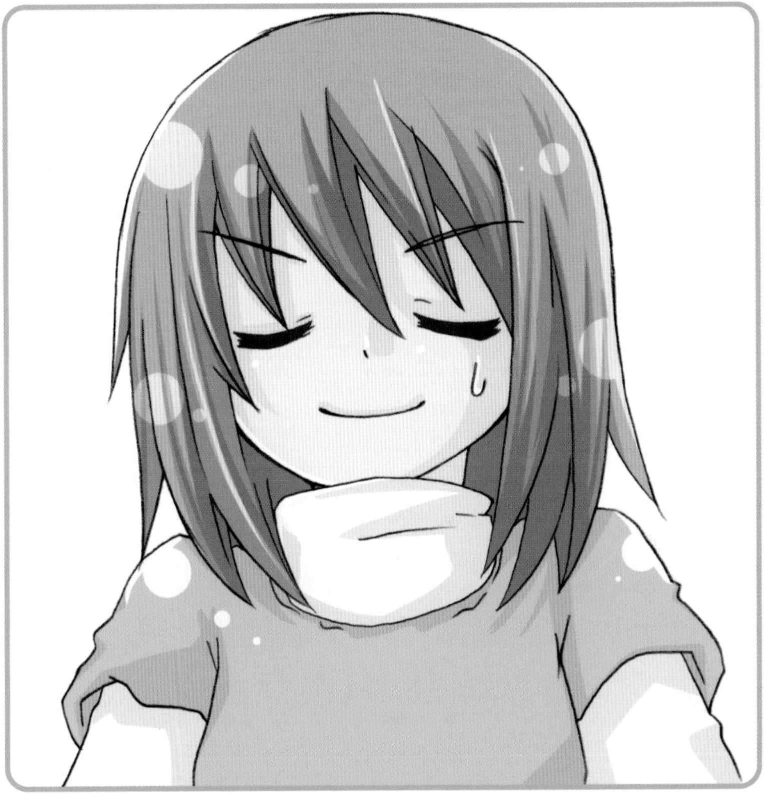

Disappointed
がっかり Gakkari

Osoi yo!

You're late!

Eiga misokonatta.

We missed the movie.

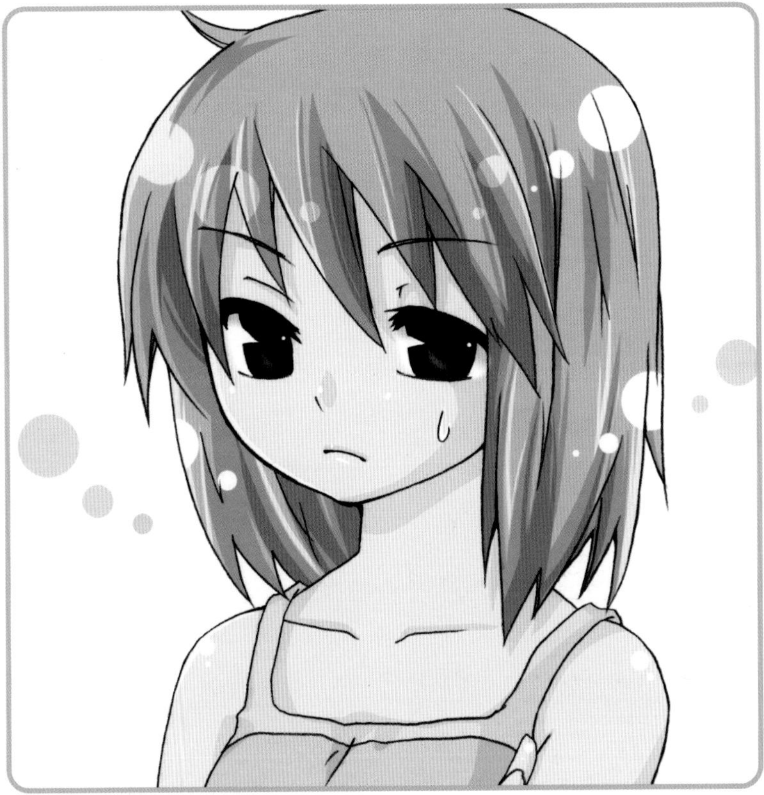

Perky

げんき Genki

O-genki desu ka?

How are you doing?

Genki da yo!

I feel great!

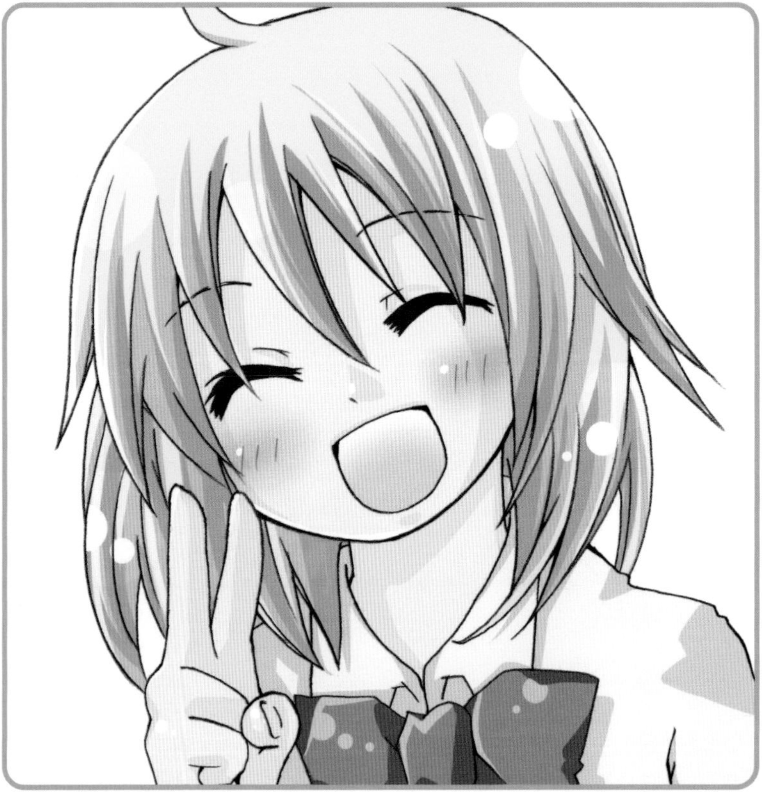

Gloomy

くらい Kurai

Watashi wa nani...

Nani mo chanto dekinai.

Woe is me...

I can't do anything right.

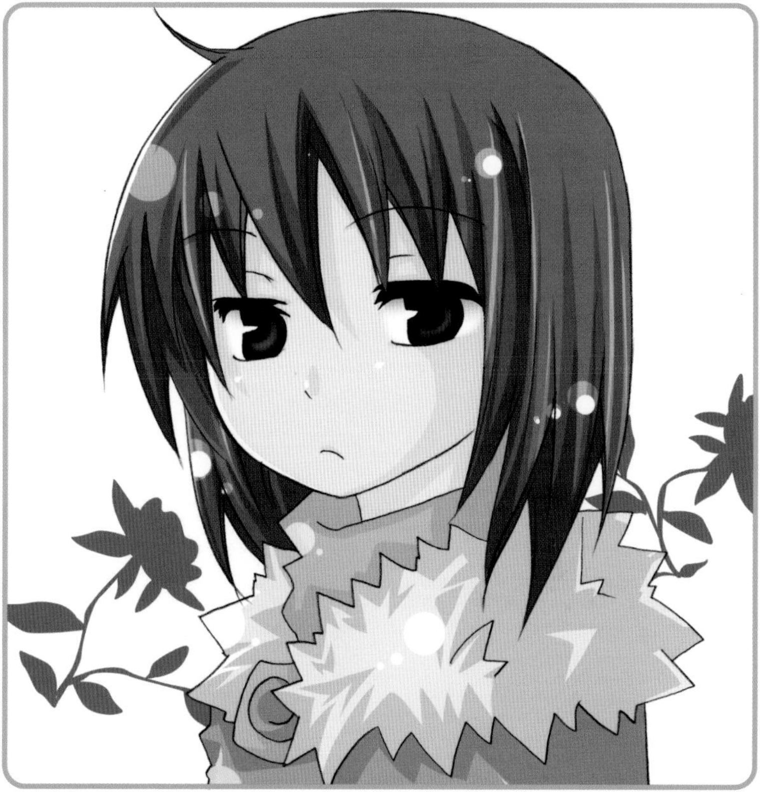

Sneaky

いじわる Ijiwaru

Fu fu fu....

Heh-heh-heh...

Ii koto kangaeta!

I've got a plan!

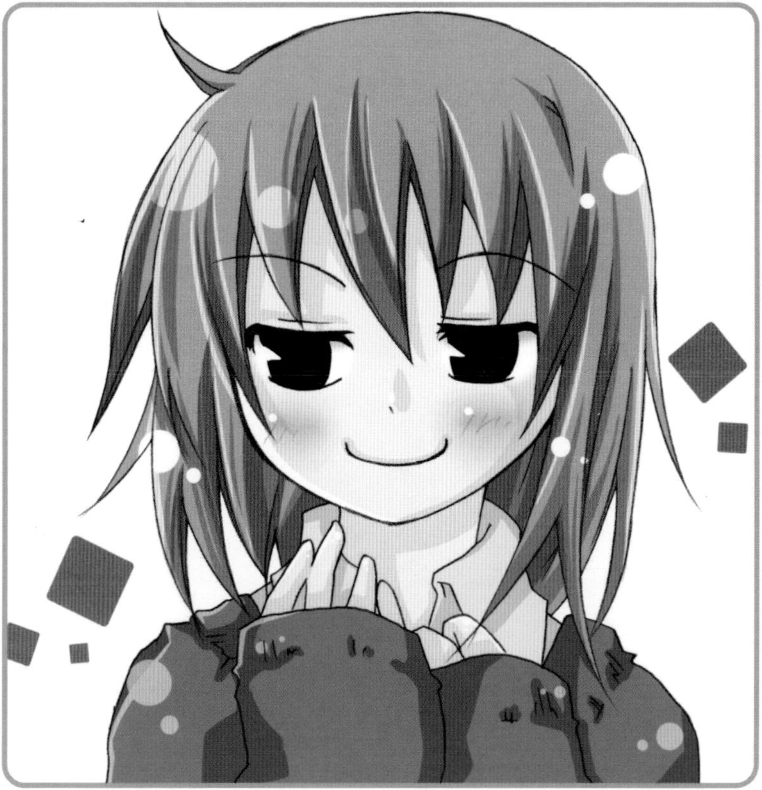

Jumpy

ばれた Bareta

Chotto!

Hey!

Odokasanaide yo!

Don't sneak up on me like that!

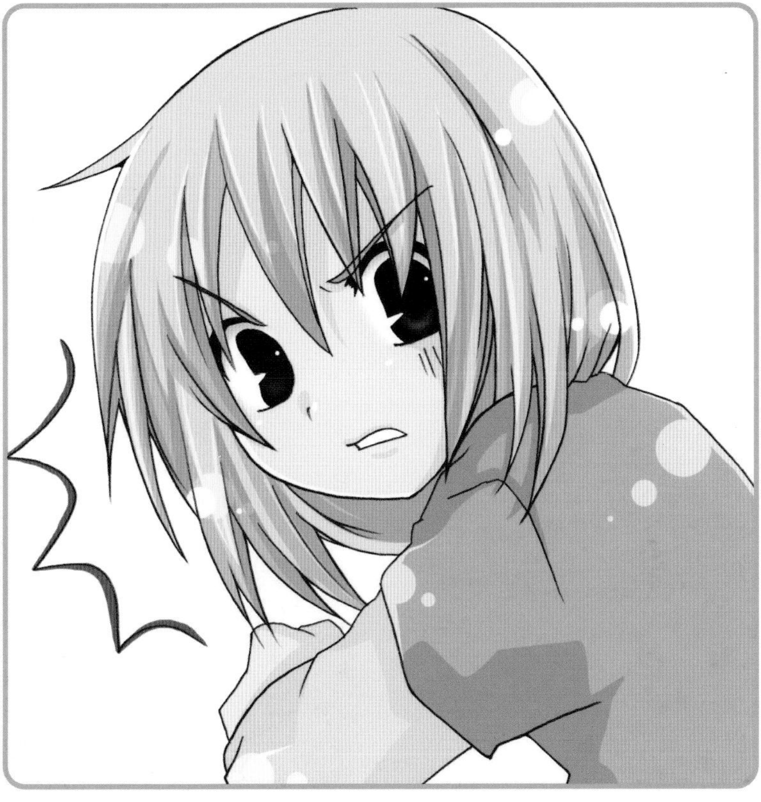

Embarrassed
はずかしい Hazukashii

Sumimasen...

I'm so sorry...

Anata no namae wasuremashita.

I've forgotten your name.

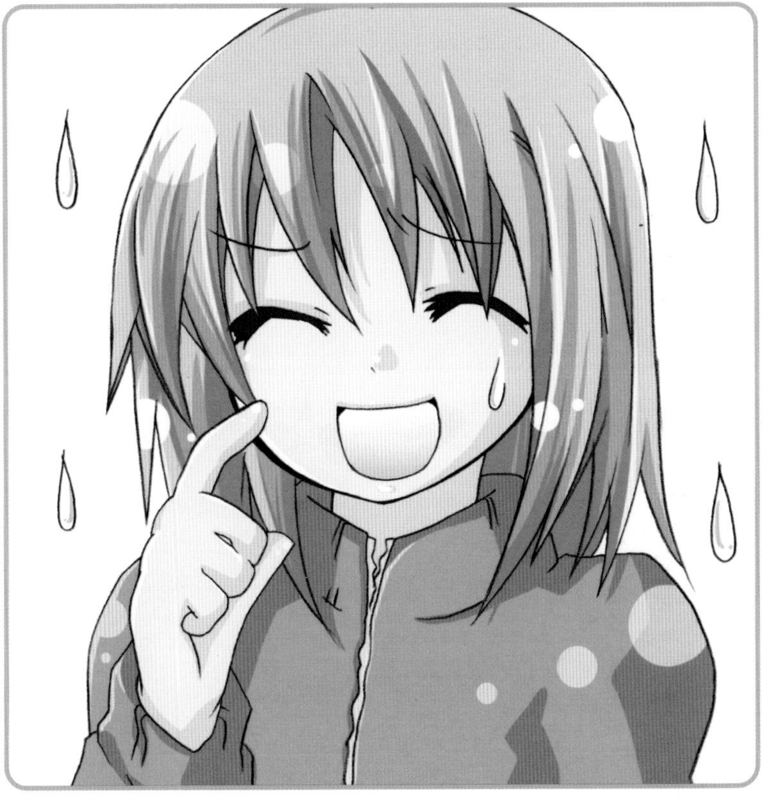

Angry
おこりっぽい Okorippoi

Jōdan deshō?

Are you kidding?

Watashi no hō ga kanojo yori kawaii yo!

I'm MUCH cuter than she is!

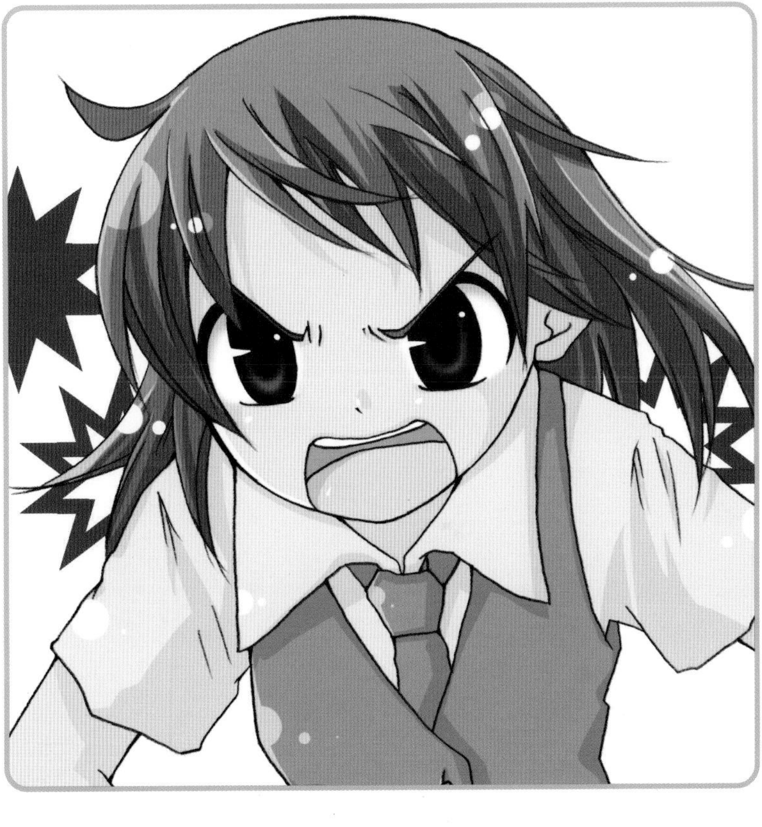

Dumbstruck

ぼんやり Bonyari

Takarakuji
atatta no?

I won the lottery?

. . . .

(Speechless)

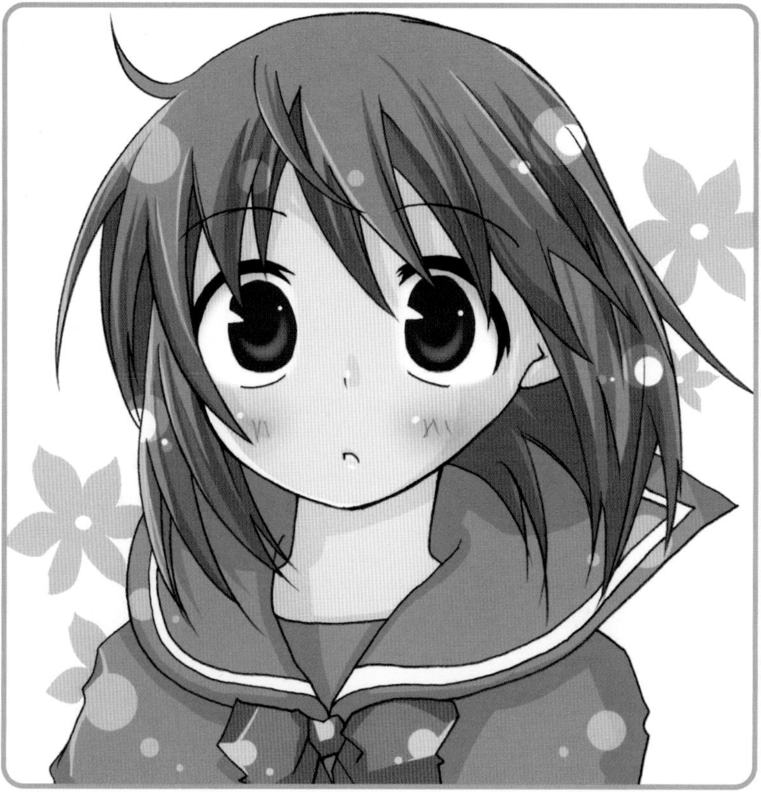

Troubled

やっかい Yakkai

Kare kanningu–
shita no ne.

I know he
cheated.

Sensei ni itta
hō ga ii ka nā?

Should I tell
the teacher?

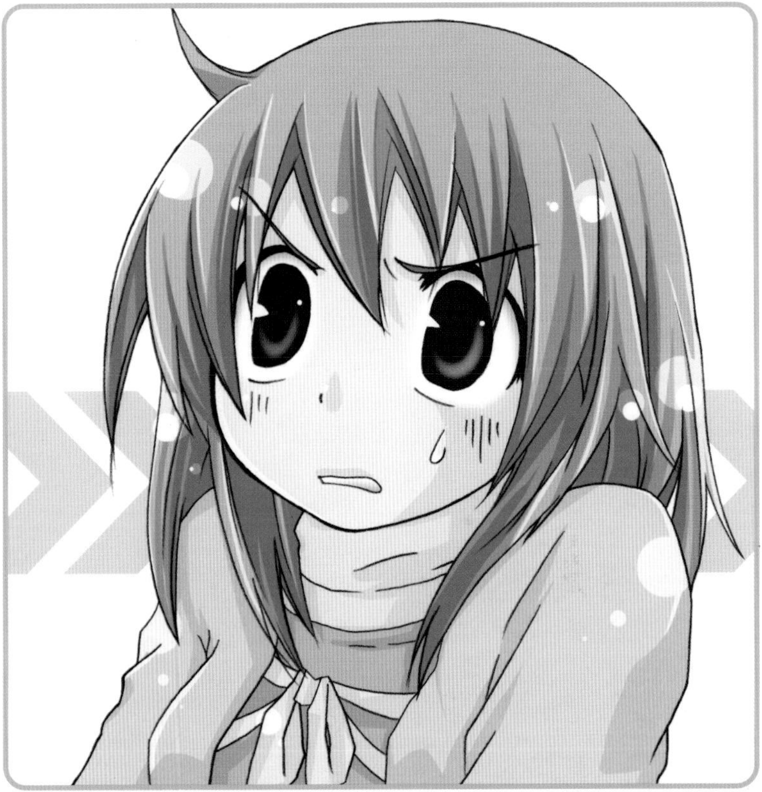

Shy

てれくさい Terekusai

Ēto... anō...

Umm... errr...

Pēji mekutte kudasai.

Please turn the page.

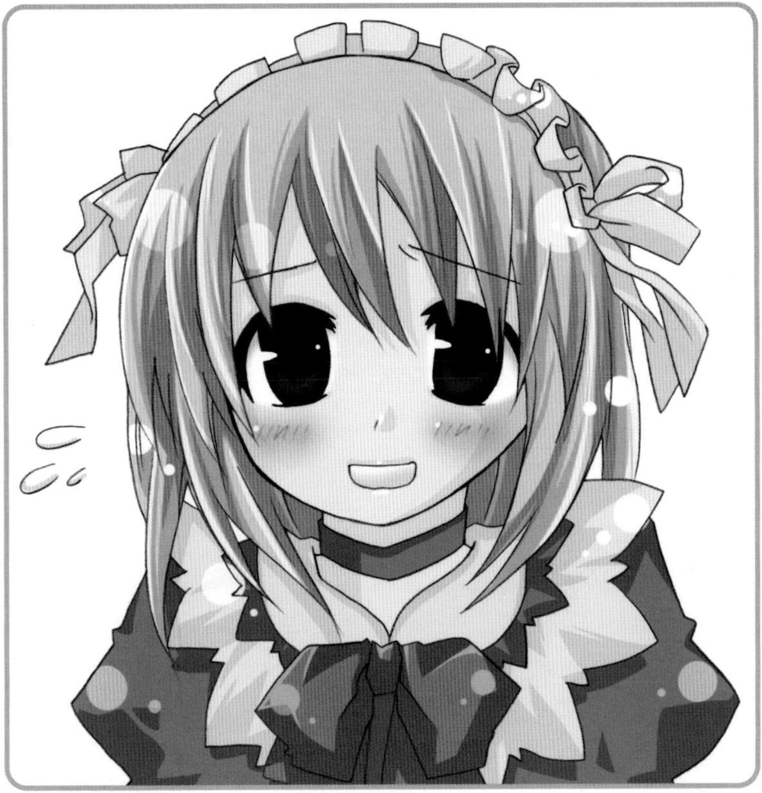

Stern

げんかく Genkaku

Kangae wa
katamarimashita.

My mind is set.

Mohaya nani mo
hanasu koto wa
arimasen.

There's nothing
left to discuss.

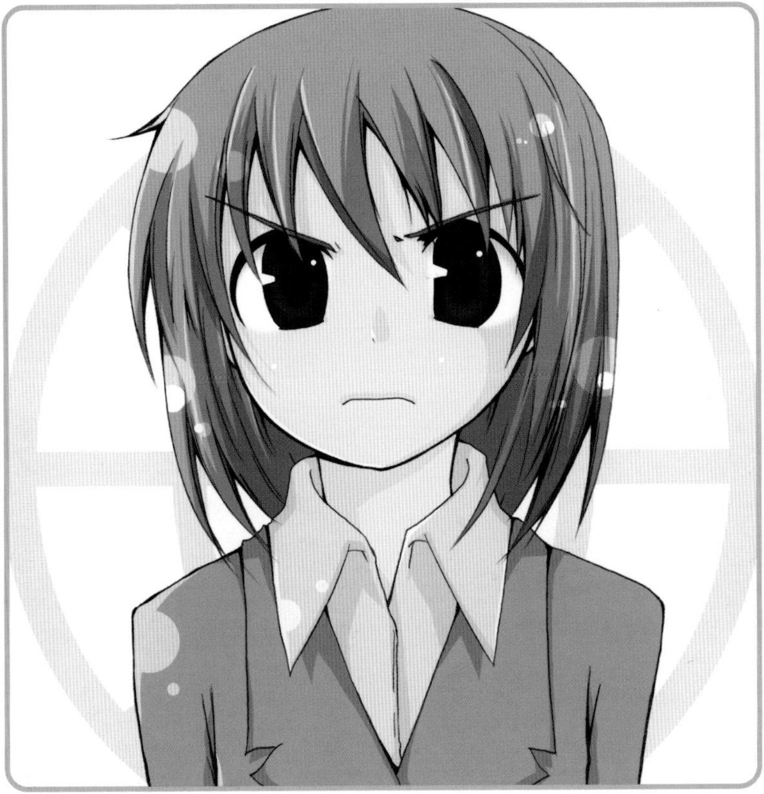

Woeful

ひさん Hisan

Haa...

Sigh...

Furareta.

Love hurts.

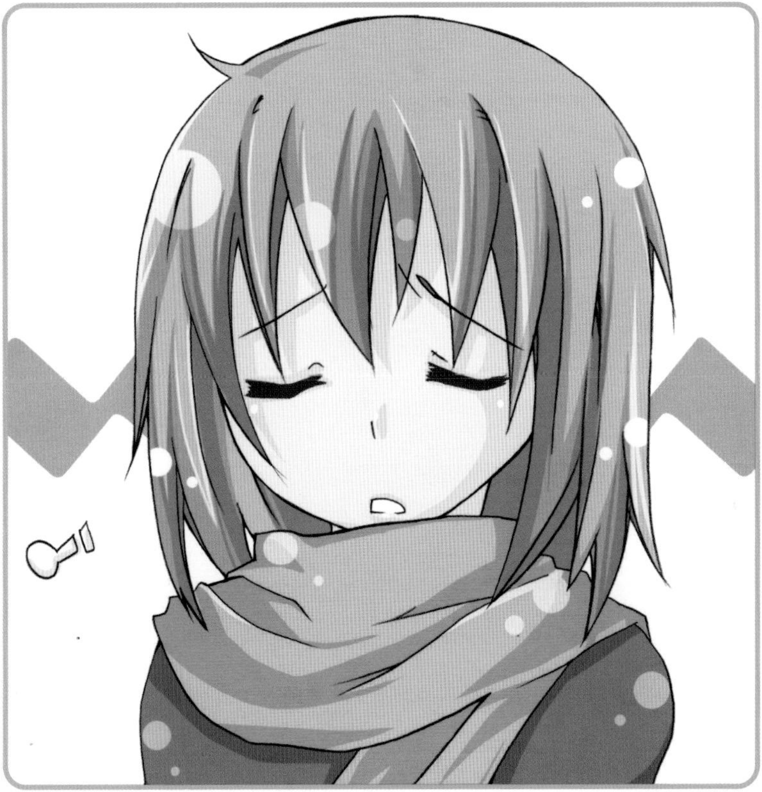

Emotional

かんじょうてき Kanjōteki

Nan demo nai yo...

Don't worry...

Ureshinamida yo.

These are tears of joy!

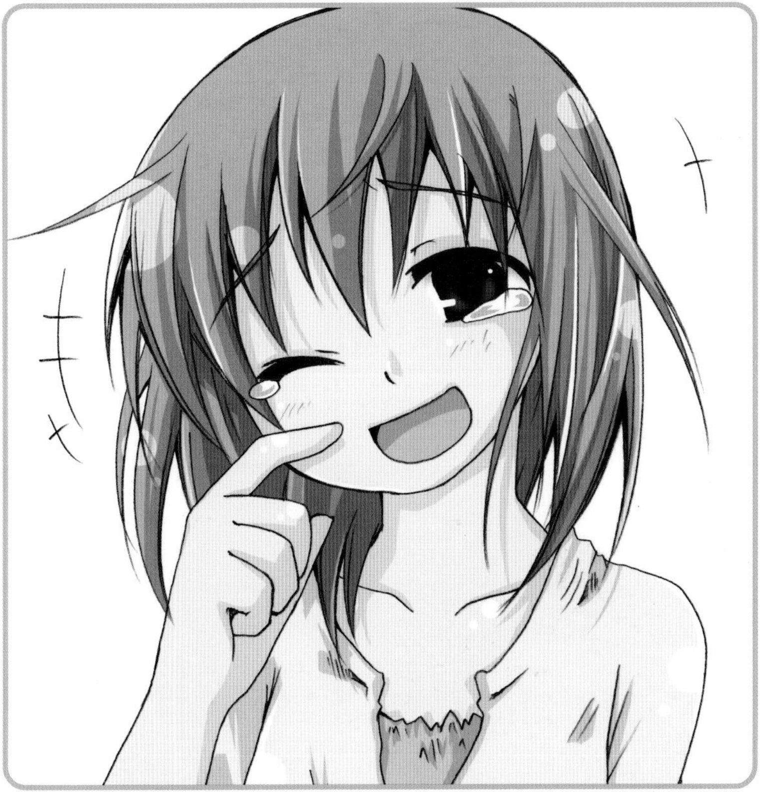

Malicious

あくい Akui

Wa ha ha ha!

Bwah-hah-hah!

Itsuka sekai o shihai suru zo!

Someday I'll rule the universe!

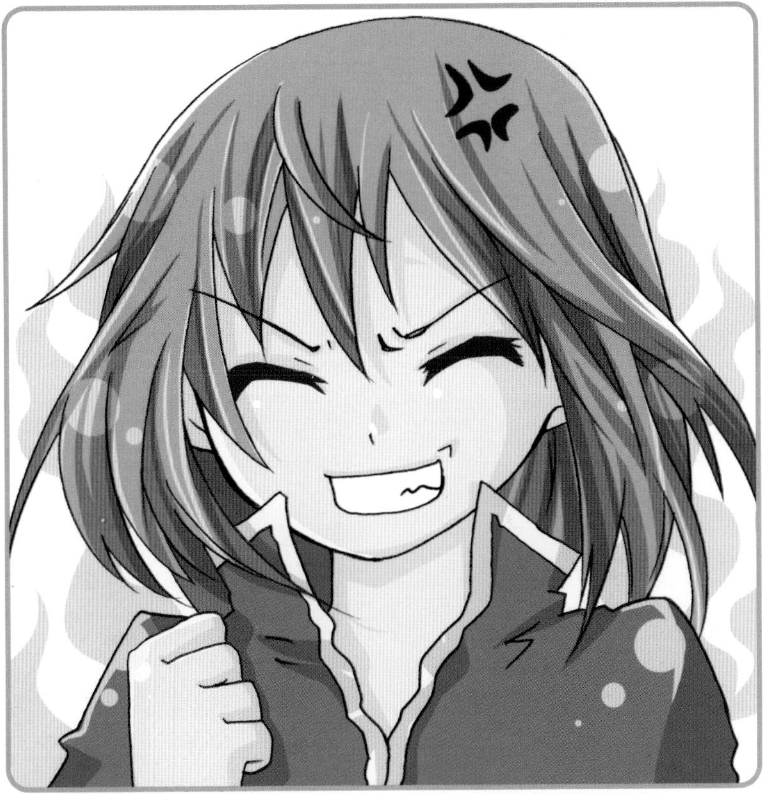

69

Doubtful

ふあん Fuan

Shiken ni
gōkakushita
ka na?

Did I pass the
test?

Iya na yokan ga
suru...

I've got a
sinking feeling...

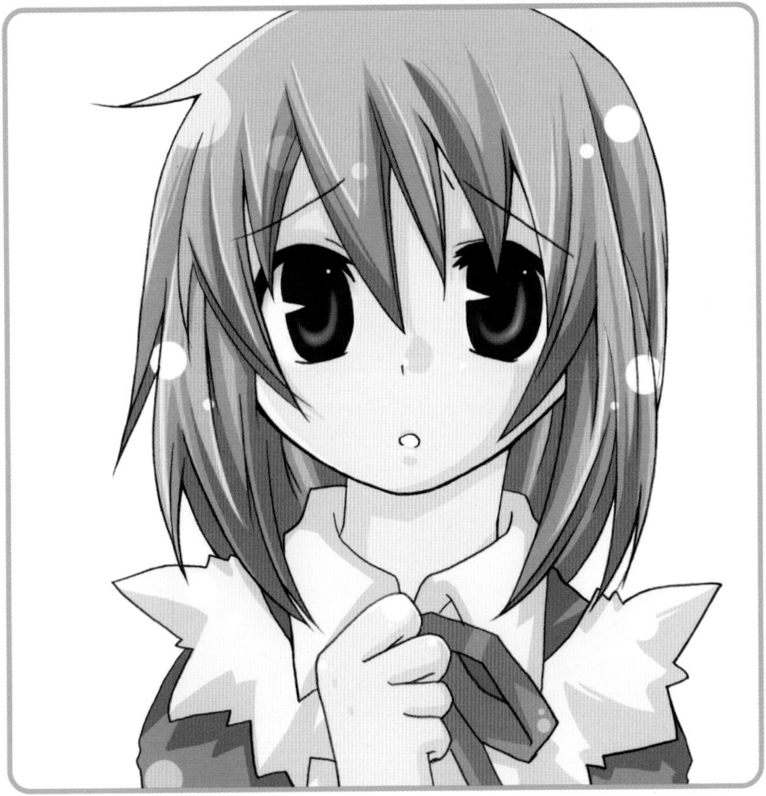

Sleepy

ねむい Nemui

Mō nemui yo.

I'm so sleepy.

Neru jikan da.

Time for bed.

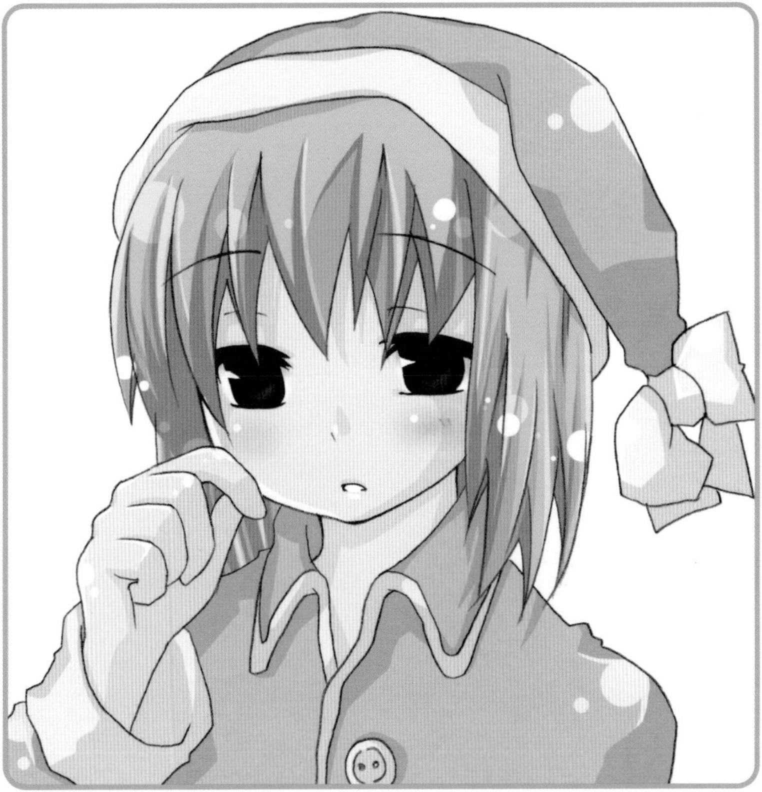

Celebratory

めでたい Medetai

Yatta!	Yokatta!
I did it!	Awesome!

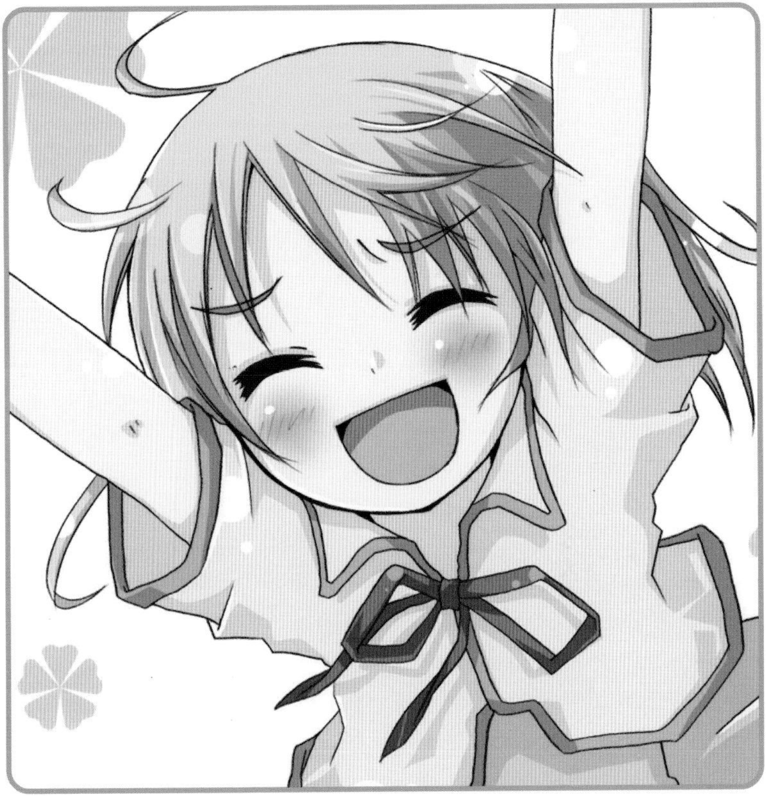

Nervous

しんけいしつ Shinkeishitsu

Basu ichatta!

I missed my bus!

Dōshiyō?

What should I do?

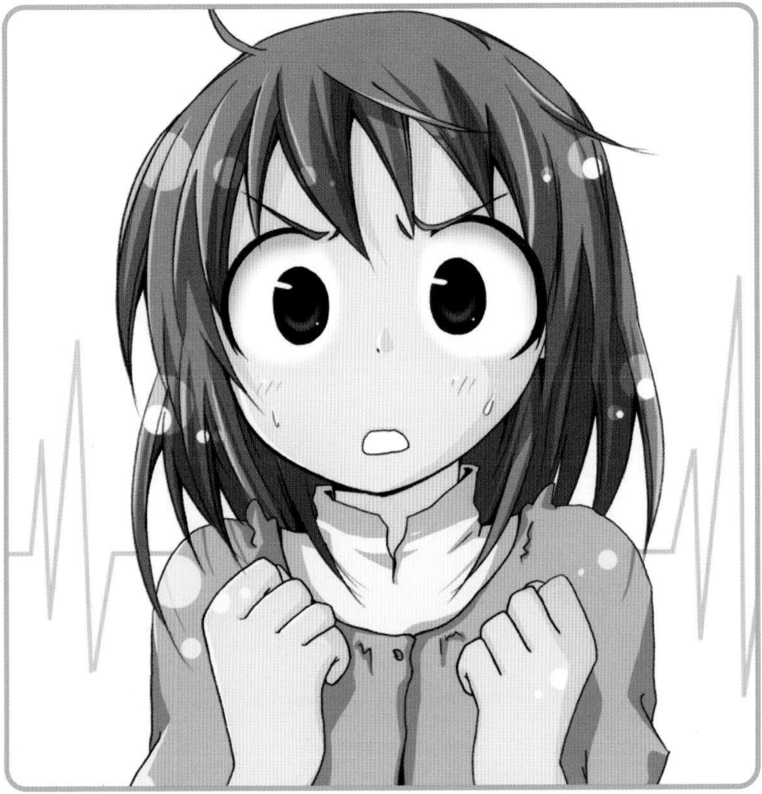

Lovesick

こいわずらい Koiwazurai

Kare kakkoii.

He's so cool.

Watashi ga ikiteru koto shitteru no kashira.

I doubt he knows I'm even alive.

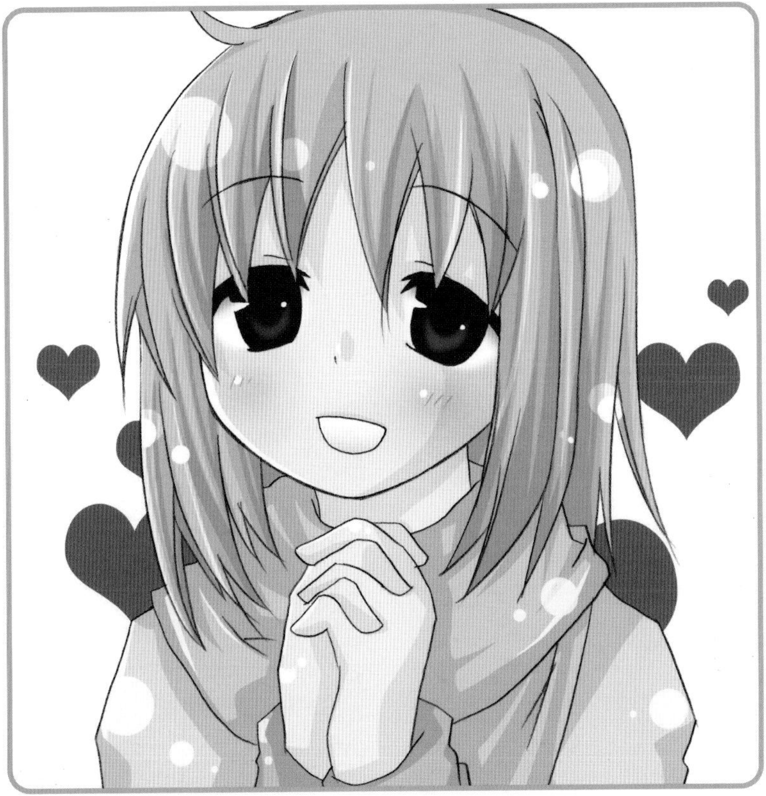

Preoccupied

みすかす Misukasu

Nani?	**Nani ka itta?**
What?	**Did you just say something?**

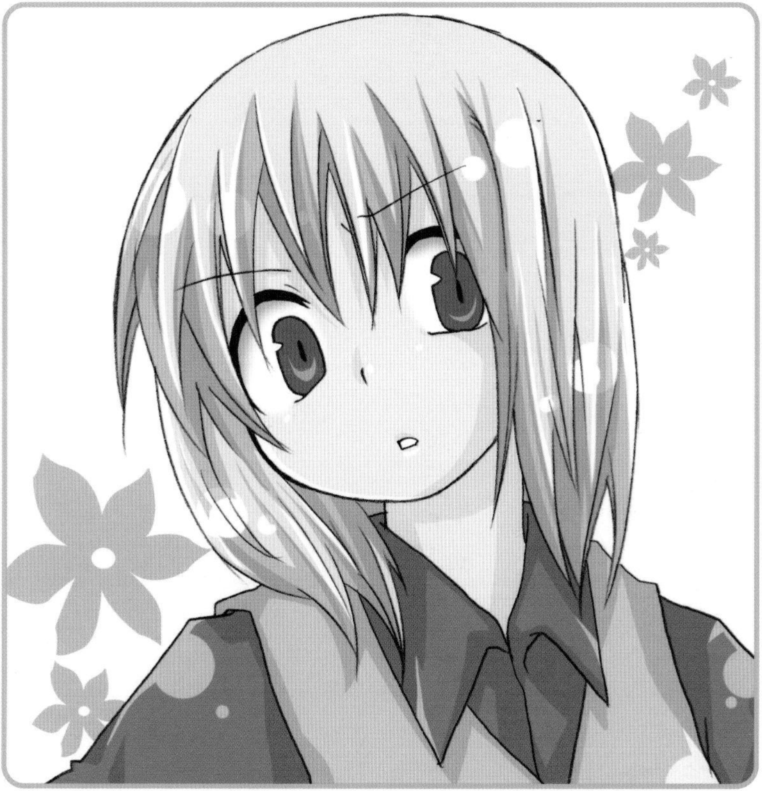

Uncomfortable

ふゆかい Fuyukai

Uu!	Ha ga itai!
Ouch!	My tooth hurts!

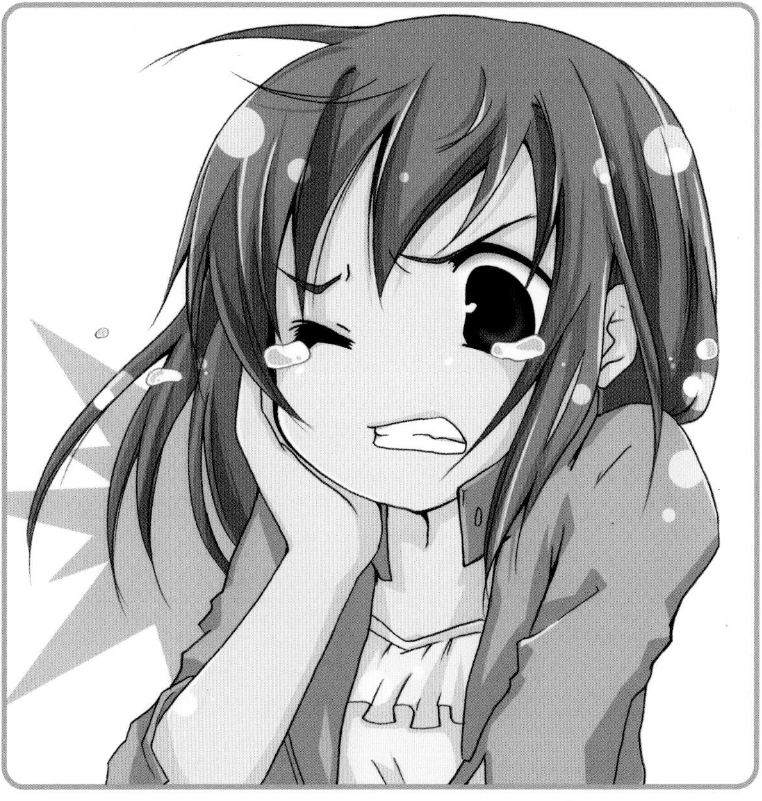

Comfortable

きもちいい Kimochi ii

Ii tenki da ne!

The weather
is lovely!

Kimochi ii!

What a great
feeling!

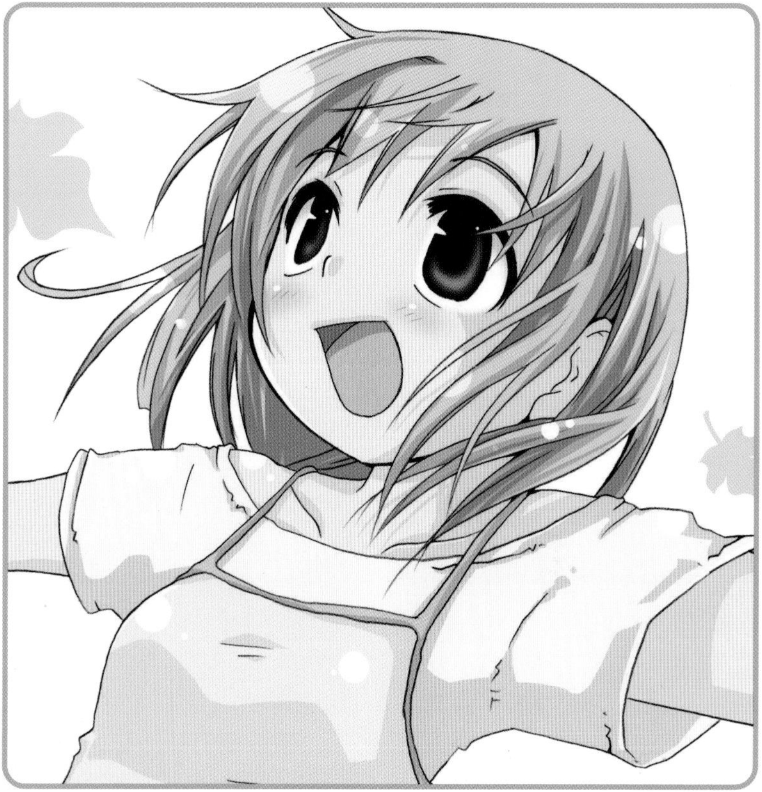

Happy
しあわせ Shiawase

Tanoshikatta!

That was fun!

Jā ne!

See you later!

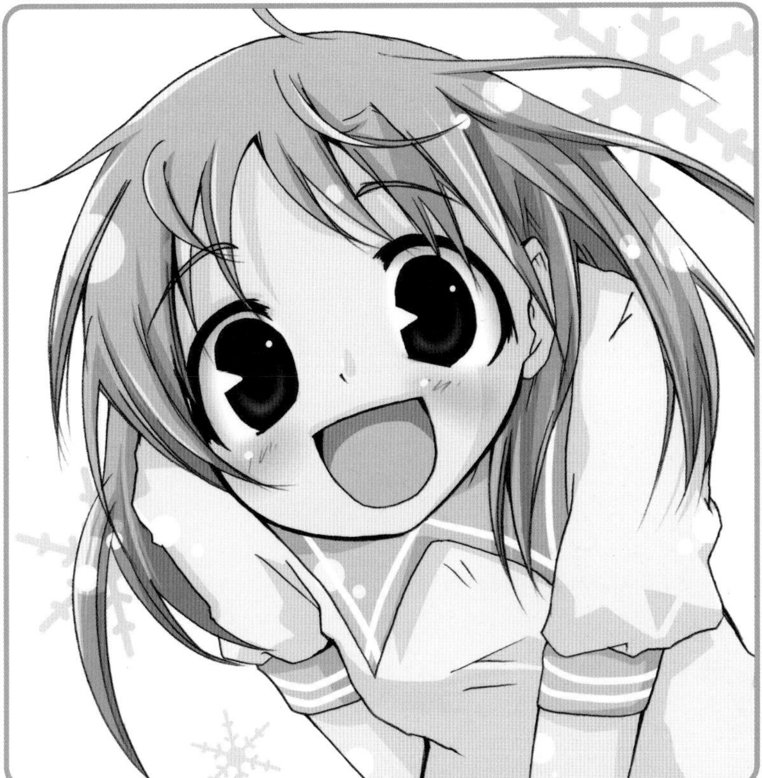

Asleep

ねむっている Nemutteiru

Oyasumi nasai.

Good night.

Yoi yume o.

Sweet dreams.

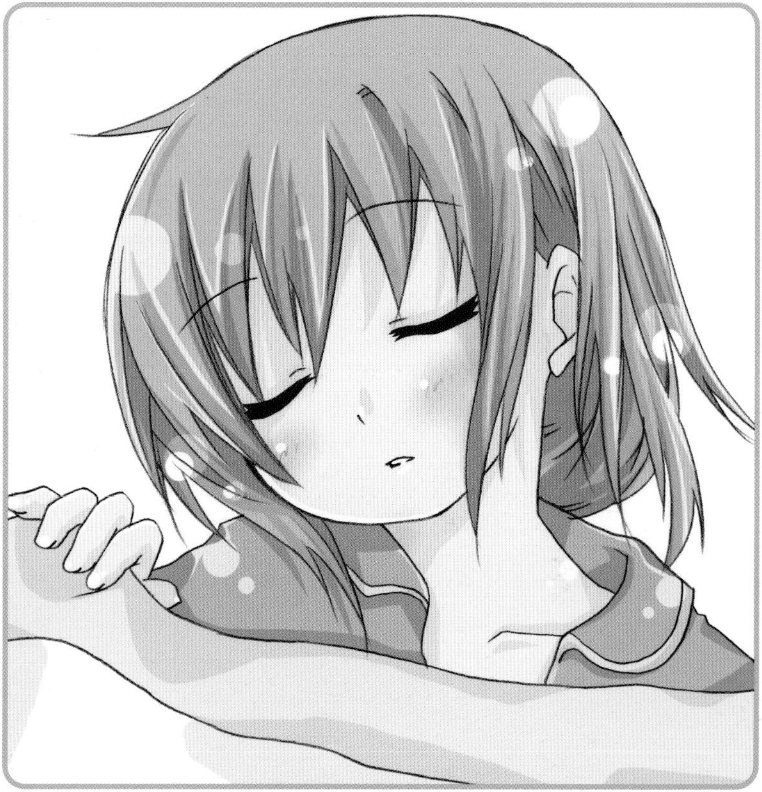

h i r a g a n a

The Japanese writing system consists of three scripts: *hiragana*, which is used for phonetic spellings of Japanese words, as well as participles, prefixes and suffixes; *katakana*, for words of foreign origin; and *kanji*, the complex Chinese characters that represent the vast majority of words used in Japanese. (When the language is romanized, as it is in this book, it is said to be written in *romaji*.)

Japanese translations of the mood keywords (happy, sad, perky, grumpy, etc.) in this book are written in both hiragana and romaji. The chart on the opposite page shows the 46 basic hiragana characters, while the charts on pages 92 and 93 feature modified hiragana sounds.

Manga enthusiasts who want to learn more about hiragana, katakana and kanji should ask their local bookstores for *Kana de Manga* (ISBN 4-921205-01-9) and *Kanji de Manga Volume 1* (ISBN 4-921205-02-7), both published by Manga University.

あ a	い i	う u	え e	お o
か ka	き ki	く ku	け ke	こ ko
さ sa	し shi	す su	せ se	そ so
た ta	ち chi	つ tsu	て te	と to
な na	に ni	ぬ nu	ね ne	の no
は ha	ひ hi	ふ fu	へ he	ほ ho
ま ma	み mi	む mu	め me	も mo
や ya		ゆ yu		よ yo
ら ra	り ri	る ru	れ re	ろ ro
わ wa				を o
				ん n

The 46 Basic Hiragana Characters
Each character represents one syllable.

Contracted Hiragana

A small や, ゆ or よ can be added to any hiragana character that ends in an "i" vowel (except for the character い itself) to form a contracted sound, as indicated here.

きゃ kya   きゅ kyu   きょ kyo

しゃ sha   しゅ shu   しょ sho

ちゃ cha   ちゅ chu   ちょ cho

にゃ nya   にゅ nyu   にょ nyo

ひゃ hya   ひゅ hyu   ひょ hyo

みゃ mya   みゅ myu   みょ myo

りゃ rya   りゅ ryu   りょ ryo

ぎゃ gya   ぎゅ gyu   ぎょ gyo

じゃ ja   じゅ ju   じょ jo

びゃ bya   びゅ byu   びょ byo

ぴゃ pya   ぴゅ pyu   ぴょ pyo

が ga	ぎ gi	ぐ gu	げ ge	ご go
ざ za	じ ji	ず zu	ぜ ze	ぞ zo
だ da	ぢ ji	づ zu	で de	ど do
ば ba	び bi	ぶ bu	べ be	ぼ bo
ぱ pa	ぴ pi	ぷ pu	ぺ pe	ぽ po

Two-Dash and One-Circle Hiragana

To modify the sounds of certain hiragana, the Japanese add two small dashes (called *dakuten*) or a tiny circle (called a *handakuten*) to the characters, as shown above.

SAORI TAKARAI is a graduate of Nippon Engineering College in Tokyo, where she studied art and graphic design.

Her illustrations have been featured in several publications, including *Shogakusei no Manga Hougen Jiten* (Children's Manga Dictionary; Gakken, 2004); *Shogakusei no Kotowaza Jiten* (Children's Dictionary of Proverbs; Sekaibunka, 2005); and Manga University's own *Kanji de Manga Special Box Set* (Japanime, 2005).

Most of the time, she's in a good mood.

MANGA UNIVERSITY

Gift Books

TOKYO   SAN FRANCISCO

ORDERING INFORMATION

Visit our campus store:
www.mangauniversity.com

Send us an email:
info@mangauniversity.com

Call us toll-free in the USA:
1-877-BUY-MANGA (877-289-6264)